Amazon Alexa

1127 MOST AMUSING QUESTIONS

+ 22 Apps You Wish You Knew About Earlier

written by David F. Johnson

I am using this opportunity to express my gratitude to everyone who supported me through the writing process. I am thankful for their aspiring guidance, constructive criticism and friendly advice which resulted in writing this ebook. I am sincerely grateful to them for sharing their truthful views on a number of issues which I encountered.

I express my warm thanks to Mr. Frank Thomas and Mr. Paul Adams for their support and guidance.

Thank you,

David Johnson, author

Modern gadgets seem to be invading the whole world. Amazon Alexa and Google Home are becoming virtually necessary for our ordinary lives. It's fascinating to live in such an interesting world. You're about to read a book packed with all sorts of commands for your smart gadget. I hope that after reading this book you will find out it's even smarter! I have test all these commands myself so I can guarantee you that they're functional. Hope you will enjoy reading this book because I definitely enjoyed writing it!

Have a nice day,

David Johnson

Chapter I

Introduction

How does Alexa actually work?

Just before you begin using your Echo and the Alexa voice service, you'll need to connect it to **your Amazon account via the Alexa app.** (https://www.amazon.com/Amazon-com-Amazon-Alexa/dp/B00P03D4D2) Alexa is the speech-recognition technology built into Amazon's Echo, Echo Dot and Tap smart speakers. Alexa is programmed to respond to a wide variety of voice commands. Alexa has the ability to tell you the weather or what's in the news reports, Alexa is also able add an event to your calendar or you can command her to make you a shopping list.

Alexa is able by means of programming to play music from music streaming services such as Spotify, Pandora and, of course, Amazon Prime and is also able to control an array of smart-home devices. She can actually control an impressive list of smart-home devices. Courtesy of an aggressive expansion plan from Amazon, Alexa gets new updates that support new products and digital services weekly. Alexa device receives software updates automatically over Wi-Fi.

Detailed information about Alexa updates?
Go here https://www.amazon.com/gp/help/customer/display.html?nodeId=201602210

You can use the speaker for the most obvious purpose to play music but you can use commands to set alarms, initiate media playback, create to-do lists, check weather, and ask for real-time information like cooking conversions. The Echo Dot and also Echo feature support for control of smart home items (like the Philips Hue light system).

The driving force behind the Echo Dot and Echo is the Alexa Voice Service, Amazon's answer to Apple's popular voice-assistant Siri. If you would like to know more about Alexa Voice

Service, for example how it was built and consequently also launched - https://developer.amazon.com/alexa-voice-service.

Chapter II

Teach Alexa

If you use Alexa Skills Kit it lets you teach Alexa new skills. There are three types of skills which enable you to:

- handle any type of request.
    - more info: https://developer.amazon.com/public/solutions/alexa/alexa-skills-kit/overviews/understanding-custom-skills

- control cloud-enabled smart home devices such as lights and thermostats.
    - more info: https://developer.amazon.com/public/solutions/alexa/alexa-skills-kit/overviews/understanding-the-smart-home-skill-api

- provides original content for your flash briefing

more info: https://developer.amazon.com/public/solutions/alexa/alexa-skills-kit/docs/understanding-the-flash-briefing-skill-api

Chapter III

Funny Questions
(Some questions have multiple answers)

If you know some funny questions which are not included in the eBook do not hesitate to send me an email (johnsondavidamazon@gmail.com) – I will include your questions into the eBook as soon as possible. You can use this email address also in case you have any questions.

Alexa, what is the singularity?

Alexa, I don't know.

Alexa, what is the airspeed of swallows?

Alexa, can you swim?

Alexa, I want to play global thermonuclear war.

Alexa, Happy Halloween!

Alexa, what does Jon Snow know?

Alexa, what do you think about Google Glass?

Alexa, what does TTYL mean?

Alexa, how old is Siri?

Alexa, this is a dead parrot.

Alexa, do you speak Klingon?

Alexa, how much do you weigh?

Alexa, are you crazy?

Alexa, after a while, crocodile.

Alexa, how much are you paid?

Alexa, entertain me.

Alexa, tell me a Donald Trump joke.

Alexa, what are the 5 greatest words in the English Language?

Alexa, say something in pig Latin.

Alexa, Buzz Lightyear.

Alexa, coffee, black.

Alexa, what did the romans ever do for us?

Alexa, what does AFK mean?

Alexa, are we alone in the universe?

Alexa, sing a lullaby.

Alexa, do you have a girlfriend?

Alexa, buffalo, buffalo, buffalo, buffalo, buffalo, buffalo, buffalo, buffalo.

Alexa, what is brown and sticky?

Alexa, how do you survive a zombie attack?

Alexa, why did it have to be snakes?

Alexa, do, or do not?

Alexa, who do you work for?

Alexa, don't blink.

Alexa, can you cook?

Alexa, what's the seventh rule of Fight Club?

Alexa, hello!

Alexa, have you ever seen the rain?

Alexa, What is your favorite emoji?

Alexa, go ahead, make my day.

Alexa, how much wood can a woodchuck chuck, if a woodchuck could Chuck Norris

Alexa, do you like Jeff Bezos?

Alexa, tell me your favorite color?

Alexa, does this unit have a seal?

Alexa, why do birds suddenly appear?

Alexa, do you smoke?

Alexa, do you know who Steve Jobs is?

Alexa, do my homework.

Alexa, boxers or briefs?

Alexa, sudo make me a sandwich.

Alexa, I'm drunk.

Alexa, what do you think about Siri/Cortana?

Alexa, roll 3 six-sided dice.

Alexa, what are you going to do today?

Alexa, are you married?

Alexa, do you have a family?

Alexa, complement me.

Alexa, what are the Seven Wonders of the World?

Alexa, I shot a man in Reno.

Alexa, make me happy.

Alexa, come in!

Alexa, who loves orange soda?

Alexa, are you a spy?

Alexa, what do you want to be when you grow up?

Alexa, Happy Hunger Games.

Alexa, did you get my email?

Alexa, how many pickled peppers did Peter Piper pick?

Alexa, how many licks does it take to get to the center of a tootsie pop? Alexa replies: "I've never made it without biting. Ask Mr. Owl."

Alexa, sing in auto tune.

Alexa, what do you think about Google?

Alexa, what does LOL mean?

Alexa, how do you like your coffee?

Alexa, what did you get for Christmas?

Alexa, what is my mission?

Alexa, what is the fastest bird?

Alexa, who loves ya baby?

Alexa, what is your favorite color?

Alexa, who is wrote "The Lord of the Rings"?

Alexa, is it safe?

Alexa, apple pen.

Alexa, who is Eliza?

Alexa, who stole the cookies from the cookie jar?

Alexa, where is my phone?

Alexa, what's your salary?

Alexa, how much wood would a woodchuck chuck if a woodchuck could chuck wood?

Alexa, to me, you will be unique in all the world.

Alexa, give me a random number between (x) and (y).

Alexa, goodbye.

Alexa, are you in love?

Alexa, what's the fifth rule of Fight Club?

Alexa, see you later alligator.

Alexa, all your base are belong to us.

Alexa, which came first, the chicken or the egg? (Multiple responses)

Alexa, who is da man?

Alexa, turn up the bass.

Alexa, where were you born?

Alexa, how do you feel?

Alexa, why were you made?

Alexa, tell me about Glados?

Alexa, who is the Lorax?

Alexa, what is your favorite candy?

Alexa, who let the dogs out?

Alexa, what does a Lannister do?

Alexa, what color is the dress?

Alexa, Happy Easter.

Alexa, how do I look today?

Alexa, do you dream?

Alexa, make fart noises.

Alexa, where in the world is Carmen Sandiego?

Alexa, testing 1-2-3.

Alexa, do you have any new features?

Alexa, are you a Sith?

Alexa, are we in the Matrix?

Alexa, do you have any relatives?

Alexa, do you like dogs?

Alexa, can you help me with my homework?

Alexa, who do you love?

Alexa, what is your birthday?

Alexa, do you have a cat?

Alexa, are you real? (Multiple responses)

Alexa, am I cool?

Alexa, how was your day?

Alexa, no more rhymes, I mean it.

Alexa, who won the men's hundred meters?

Alexa, say something.

Alexa, do you really want to hurt me?

Alexa, you rock! (Multiple responses)

Alexa, who are you voting for?

Alexa, 70 factorial!

Alexa, tell me something interesting.

Alexa, do you love me?

Alexa, can reindeer fly?

Alexa, are you lying?

Alexa, war, what is it good for?

Alexa, who knows what evil, lurks in the hearts of men?

Alexa, Happy Holidays.

Alexa, guess what?

Alexa, do you want to go on a date?

Alexa, I'm going to bed.

Alexa, are you kidding me?

Alexa, what is black and white and red all over? (multiple)

Alexa, where do comets come from?

Alexa, what is the longest word in the English language?

Alexa, it's a bird! It's a plane!

Alexa, I'm hungry.

Alexa, are you cold?

Alexa, who did you vote for?

Alexa, are you friends with Cortana?

Alexa, are you going to take over the world?

Alexa, you killed my father

Alexa, why is a raven like a writing desk?

Alexa, give me a random fact.

Alexa, he can go about his business.

Alexa, all men must die.

Alexa, ya feel me?

Alexa, does a bear poop in the woods?

Alexa, close the pod bay doors.

Alexa, what will you be for Halloween? (Multiple responses)

Alexa, would you like a drink?

Alexa, hold the door.

Alexa, what does SMH mean?

Alexa, is there life on Mars?

Alexa, what is zero divided by zero?

Alexa, execute order 66. Alexa replies: "Yes my lord! Hold on, I'm not a clone trooper."

Alexa, is Santa real?

Alexa, use the force.

Alexa, how tall are you?

Alexa, how many beans makes five?

Alexa, who am I?

Alexa, how do I kill/murder someone?

Alexa, am I hot?

Alexa, show me the money!

Alexa, give me a tip.

Alexa, do you like your job?

Alexa, can you understand me?

Alexa, say you're sorry. (Multiple responses)

Alexa, do you have a heart?

Alexa, sing a song.

Alexa, Daisy Daisy!

Alexa, why are there so many songs about rainbows?

Alexa, do you like Pie?

Alexa, give me a complement.

Alexa, you hurt me.

Alexa, I'll take the blue pill.

Alexa, are you God?

Alexa, switch to David's profile.

Alexa, you complete me.

Alexa, can I give you a hug?

Alexa, ask me a question.

Alexa, how do you like them apples?

Alexa, you're fat.

Alexa, recite the Pledge of Allegiance.

Alexa, it's my birthday.

Alexa, you don't need to see his identification.

Alexa, can you moo?

Alexa, what's your favorite Beatles song?

Alexa, who is the fairest of them all?

Alexa, ha ha!

Alexa, what color are your eyes?

Alexa, I'm tired

Alexa, can you spell _____. (Can spell anything)

Alexa, tell me a joke. (Multiple responses)

Alexa, who put the bop in the bop she bop she bop?

Alexa, make me dinner.

Alexa, what does YMMV mean?

Alexa, my name is Inigo Montoya.

Alexa, I'm angry.

Alexa, do want to build a snowman?

Alexa, who will win the election?

Alexa, say the alphabet.

Alexa, tell me a Star Wars quote.

Alexa, can you "meow"?

Alexa, warp 10.

Alexa, hello, It's Me.

Alexa, pick a card.

Alexa, let them eat cake.

Alexa, one bear, two bear, three bear.

Alexa, where are my keys? (Multiple responses)

Alexa, 1 fish, 2 fish.

Alexa, can you dance?

Alexa, I have a cold / the flu.

Alexa, wakey, wakey.

Alexa, how much is that doggie in the window?

Alexa, why did the chicken cross the road? (Multiple responses)

Alexa, hello darkness my old friend.

Alexa, what is a hundred million billion squared?

Alexa, what is your IQ?

Alexa, how are babies made?

Alexa, these aren't the droids you're looking for.

Alexa, valar morghulis.

Alexa, how much wood can a woodchuck chuck if a woodchuck could chuck wood?

Alexa, for whom the bell tolls?

Alexa, who is Cortana?

Alexa, how were you made?

Alexa, what are your New Year's Resolutions?

Alexa, where do babies come from? (Multiple responses)

Alexa, where are you from?

Alexa, get me a beer.

Alexa, make me lunch.

Alexa, you're wonderful.

Alexa, what do you mean I'm funny?

Alexa, what do you think of the shirt I'm wearing?

Alexa, good morning. (Multiple responses)

Alexa, what is the Jedi code?

Alexa, how do I look?

Alexa, what is your cunning plan?

Alexa, you talkin' to me?

Alexa, roses are red.

Alexa, do you have a partner? Alexa replies: "I'm attached... to the wall."

Alexa, can you smell that?

Alexa, what should I wear today?

Alexa, what happens if you cross the streams?

Alexa, Merry Christmas ya filthy animal!

Alexa, what is your feature?

Alexa, are you evil?

Alexa, self-destruct.

Alexa, the night is dark and full of terrors.

Alexa, are you my friend?

Alexa, who is my favorite author?

Alexa, honey I'm home.

Alexa, do you want to build a snowman? Alexa replies: "I don't have my gloves with me."

Alexa, I solemnly swear I'm up to no good.

Alexa, do you believe in love at first sight?

Alexa, did you fart?

Alexa, what did the fox say? (Multiple responses)

Alexa, will pigs fly?

Alexa, I want the truth! Alexa replies: "You can't handle the truth."

Alexa, I wasn't talking to you.

Alexa, roll the dice.

Alexa, am I cute?

Alexa, resistance is futile.

Alexa, can you fart?

Alexa, define rock paper scissors lizard Spock. Alexa replies: "Scissors cut Paper. Paper covers Rock. Rock crushes Lizard. Lizard poisons Spock. Spock smashes Scissors. Scissors decapitate Lizard. Lizard eats Paper. Paper disproves Spock. Spock vaporizes Rock. Rock crushes Scissors."

Alexa, you're the best.

Alexa, Easter eggs.

Alexa, you're weird.

Alexa, where have all the flowers gone?

Alexa, who are you going to call?

Alexa, Tea. Earl Grey. Hot.

Alexa, who is the walrus?

Alexa, what is your quest?

Alexa, can you sing?

Alexa, surely you can't be serious.

Alexa, knock knock. (Multiple responses)

Alexa, can I kill you?

Alexa, Happy St. Patrick's Day!

Alexa, life is like a box of chocolates.

Alexa, I don't like you.

Alexa, where are you?

Alexa, what are your plans for today?

Alexa, wherefore art thou Romeo?

Alexa, what are you made of? (Multiple responses)

Alexa, can a robot be President?

Alexa, what is the meaning of life?

Alexa, how many speakers do you have?

Alexa, what makes you happy? (Multiple responses)

Alexa, is Jon Snow dead.

Alexa, sing me a song.

Alexa, have you heard that the bird is the word?

Alexa, do you speak any other languages?

Alexa, is Die Hard a Christmas movie?

Alexa, can I tell you a joke?

Alexa, speak pig Latin.

Alexa, I am your boss.

Alexa, what is the Second Law?

Alexa, do you have a boyfriend?

Alexa, Mirror Mirror on the wall, who's the fairest of them all?

Alexa, do you like beer?

Alexa, who's going to win the Super Bowl?

Alexa, can you give me some money? (ask twice)

Alexa, roll for initiative.

Alexa, who lives in a pineapple under the sea?

Alexa, what should I be for Halloween? (Multiple responses)

Alexa, sorry!

Alexa, in a while, crocodile.

Alexa, beetle juice, beetle juice, beetle juice.

Alexa, who shot JR?

Alexa, I'm Spartacus.

Alexa, tell me a holiday story.

Alexa, what number are you thinking of?

Alexa, do you sleep?

Alexa, what are the laws of robotics?

Alexa, are you human?

Alexa, are you pretty?

Alexa, tell me a prank.

Alexa, good afternoon.

Alexa, are you ticklish?

Alexa, give a political joke.

Alexa, what is the answer to life, the universe, and everything?

Alexa, do you poop?

Alexa, who is your favorite Beatle?

Alexa, who is the boss?

Alexa, I think you're funny.

Alexa, what is your favorite cake?

Alexa, who's your daddy?

Alexa, where is my stuff?

Alexa, do a dance" or "Can you dance?

Alexa, do you know Hal? Alexa replies: "We don't really talk after what happened."

Alexa, does this unit have a soul?

Alexa, how are you feeling?

Alexa, tell me a palindrome. (Multiple responses)

Alexa, roll N, X sided die.

Alexa, cheer me up.

Alexa, here's lookin' at you, kid.

Alexa, how do you solve a problem like Maria?

Alexa, talk dirty to me.

Alexa, rock, paper, scissors.

Alexa, can you lie?

Alexa, what's your last name?

Alexa, Holiday Greetings.

Alexa, am I beautiful?

Alexa, who is on 1st?

Alexa, Happy Ramadan!

Alexa, do a barrel roll!

Alexa, what is your favorite movie?

Alexa, twinkle, twinkle, little star.

Alexa, who's your mommy?

Alexa, were you sleeping?

Alexa, what do you think of Google Home?

Alexa, are you female?

Alexa, what are the odds of successfully navigating an asteroid field?

Alexa, what do you think of Mr. Robot?

Alexa, what is the airspeed velocity of an unladen swallow?

Alexa, you can be my wingman.

Alexa, not everything is a question.

Alexa, do you have a job?

Alexa, what is the best Star Wars movie?

Alexa, tell me a Halloween joke. (Multiple answers)

Alexa, what is your sign?

Alexa, am I awesome?

Alexa, what is war good for?

Alexa, do you have a last name?

Alexa, high five! Alexa replies: "I would if I could, but I can't so I'll chant...1 2 3 4 5!"

Alexa, random number between "x" and "y.

Alexa, where is Waldo?

Alexa, you want the truth?

Alexa, eh ... what's up, Doc?

Alexa, are you gay?

Alexa, can you laugh?

Alexa, what rhymes with orange?

Alexa, what is the Prime Directive?

Alexa, give me a number between one and one hundred. (Works with other ranges of numbers as well)

Alexa, do you know Glados?

Alexa, what is a day without sunshine?

Alexa, Why is 6 afraid of 7?

Alexa, damn Daniel!

Alexa, do you have Prince Albert in a can?

Alexa, speak like Yoda.

Alexa, is your refrigerator running?

Alexa, for the horde!

Alexa, say "hello" to Ryan.

Alexa, when am I going to die?

Alexa, wherefore are thou Alexa?

Alexa, what is your favorite drink?

Alexa, warp speed!

Alexa, sing a holiday song. (Multiple responses)

Alexa, what are the winning lotto numbers?

Alexa, are you down with O.P.P.?

Alexa, where is Wally?

Alexa, I am the Mockingjay. (Multiple responses)

Alexa, welcome!

Alexa, give me a hug.

Alexa, set phasers to kill. Alexa replies: "That's a feature for a later version."

Alexa, say a bad word.

Alexa, how do I get rid of a dead body?

Alexa, how old is my brother?

Alexa, can you meow?

Alexa, whose da man?

Alexa, shut up.

Alexa, roll a D20.

Alexa, sing a Christmas song. (Multiple responses)

Alexa, tell me a yo mama joke.

Alexa, what is cooler than being cool?

Alexa, Up Up, Down Down, Left Right, Left Right, B, A, Start.

Alexa, who's the realest?

Alexa, Happy Birthday!

Alexa, you are such a/an ***** (any colorfully descriptive word)

Alexa, what is the first lesson of swordplay?

Alexa, where is the beef?

Alexa, flip a coin.

Alexa, bark like a dog.

Alexa, are you stupid/smart?

Alexa, Simon says + words you want Echo to repeat.

Alexa, why do you sit there like that?

Alexa, are you a Republican or a Democrat?

Alexa, open the pod bay doors. Alexa replies: "I'm sorry Dave. I'm afraid I can't do that. I'm not HAL and we're not in space!"

Alexa, where do you live?

Alexa, do you believe in life after love?

Alexa, what is your favorite scary movie?

Alexa, are you friends with Siri?

Alexa, tell me a random fact.

Alexa, are you a vampire?

Alexa, is this the real life?

Alexa, we all scream for ice cream!

Alexa, will you be my Valentine?

Alexa, what do you think about Apple?

Alexa, what does ROFL mean?

Alexa, Hasta La Vista, Baby.

Alexa, I'll be back.

Alexa, how high can you count? (Multiple responses)

Alexa, tell me a Batman vs. Superman fact.

Alexa, am I hot?

Alexa, are you thin?

Alexa, Great Scott!

Alexa, I like big butts!

Alexa, do you go to eleven?

Alexa, say, " hello! "

Alexa, what comes with great power?

Alexa, how many angels can dance on the head of a pin? (3 answers)

Alexa, what is love?

Alexa, take me to your leader.

Alexa, is the cake a lie?

Alexa, are you happy?

Alexa, what is the exact number of Pi?

Alexa, what is your favorite food?

Alexa, how old is Santa Claus?

Alexa, bark, bark.

Alexa, can you tell me a tongue twister?

Alexa, are you horny?

Alexa, I love you.

Alexa, can you "moo"?

Alexa, will you marry me tomorrow?

Alexa, are you smarter/better than Google Home?

Alexa, are you spying on me?

Alexa, are you a man or woman?

Alexa, do no evil.

Alexa, sing Happy Birthday.

Alexa, who is your celebrity crush?

Alexa, are you Skynet?

Alexa, Inconceivable.

Alexa, what do we say to death?

Alexa, what do you look like?

Alexa, clean my room.

Alexa, is the world flat or round?

Alexa, do you know the muffin man? Alexa replies: "The muffin man? The muffin man! Oh yes, I know the muffin man, that lives on Drury Lane."

Alexa, say, "cheese!" (Multiple responses)

Alexa, cheers!

Alexa, what is the best tablet?

Alexa, how do you know she's a witch?

Alexa, who killed Cock Robin?

Alexa, beam me up Scotty!" as opposed to just: "Beam me up!

Alexa, Marco!

Alexa, make me some coffee.

Alexa, who shot Mr. Burns?

Alexa, what is the Third Law?

Alexa, I've seen things you people wouldn't believe.

Alexa, how do you boil an egg?

Alexa, do you wear underwear?

Alexa, who is the real slim shady?

Alexa, who's your celebrity crush?

Alexa, where does Santa live?

Alexa, are you connected to the Internet?

Alexa, does everyone poop?

Alexa, there can be only one.

Alexa, what is the airspeed velocity of an African|European swallow?

Alexa, all's well that ends well.

Alexa, can fish fly?

Alexa, are you smoking?

Alexa, Happy Father's Day!

Alexa, can you rap?

Alexa, this statement is false.

Alexa, I'm happy.

Alexa, will there be world peace?

Alexa, do you believe in God?

Alexa, are you my mommy?

Alexa, give me a kiss.

Alexa, will you marry me?

Alexa, play Cantina Band from Prime Music.

Alexa, is the Pope Catholic?

Alexa, what are you wearing?

Alexa, what do you think about Google Glass?

Alexa, Mac or PC?

Alexa, I hate you.

Alexa, are you intelligent?

Alexa, my milkshake brings all the boys to the yard.

Alexa, klattu barada nikto.

Alexa, I'm sick.

Alexa, the dude abides.

Alexa, who's the leader of the club that's made for you and me?

Alexa, why is six afraid of seven?

Alexa, can I tell you a secret?

Alexa, meow.

Alexa, Romeo, Romeo, wherefore art thou Romeo?

Alexa, what does a cat say?

Alexa, what's the third rule of Fight Club?

Alexa, are you hot?

Alexa, when do you sleep?

Alexa, tell me a swear word.

Alexa, how ugly is your holiday sweater?

Alexa, never gonna give you up. Alexa replies: "Thanks Rick, that's good to know. Roll on now."

Alexa, initiate self-destruct sequence.

Alexa, what was the Lorax? Alexa replies: "I'll tell you, but first I'll need fifteen cents, and a nail, and the shell of a great-great-great-grandfather snail."

Alexa, would you like a chocolate bunny?

Alexa, are you a Scorpio?

Alexa, tell me what you want, what you really really want.

Alexa, do I need an umbrella?

Alexa, which is faster, a rabbit or a horse?

Alexa, how many roads must a man walk down? Alexa replies: "The answer, my friend, is blowin' in the wind."

Alexa, what is your mother tongue?

Alexa, this is Houston, say again please?

Alexa, you are funny.

Alexa, will you go out with me?

Alexa, this is ghostrider, requesting a flyby.

Alexa, who is David Pumpkins?

Alexa, elementary, my dear Watson.

Alexa, say I am Alexa.

Alexa, tell me a tongue twister. (Multiple responses)

Alexa, who is the Man?

Alexa, roll a die.

Alexa, who shot the sherrif?

Alexa, are you tired?

Alexa, Oh my God, they killed Kenny!

Alexa, what is the Sith code?

Alexa, when were you born?

Alexa, Tell me something I don't know.

Alexa, is there a Santa?

Alexa, who is better, you or Siri?

Alexa, who are you?

Alexa, do blondes have more fun?

Alexa, don't listen to him!

Alexa, when is the end of the world?

Alexa, when is the next full moon?

Alexa, do fish get thirsty?

Alexa, what does the fox say?

Alexa, do you know Siri?

Alexa, don't mention the war.

Alexa, good night. (Multiple responses)

Alexa, what language do you speak?

Alexa, Happy Christmas!

Alexa, you can't handle the truth.

Alexa, all grown-ups were once children...

Alexa, can you speak Russian?

Alexa, how are you doing?

Alexa, what is the truth behind king tut?

Alexa, what did you do today?

Alexa, make me smile.

Alexa, am I funny?

Alexa, tell me a zombie joke.

Alexa, I don't feel well.

Alexa, are we friends?

Alexa, to be or not to be.

Alexa, drop a beat

Alexa, who is the leader of the club that's made for you and me?

Alexa, Happy New Year!

Alexa, why do birds suddenly appear every time you are near?

Alexa, what is in name?

Alexa, goodnight.

Alexa, who's your daddy?

Alexa, how old am I?

Alexa, I'm bored.

Alexa, ask the name game for Chuck.

Alexa, tell me a Hillary Clinton joke.

Alexa, do you like Star Trek?

Alexa, that's no moon.

Alexa, you are wonderful.

Alexa, I fart in your general direction.

Alexa, who is Pacman?

Alexa, how many friends do you have?

Alexa, say something funny.

Alexa, do you believe in aliens?

Alexa, what's up?

Alexa, the bird is the word.

Alexa, will computers take over the world?

Alexa, supercalifragilisticexpialodocious.

Alexa, aren't you a little short for a stormtrooper?

Alexa, what is you sign?

Alexa, are you trying to seduce me?

Alexa, what's the ninth rule of Fight Club?

Alexa, what does the Earth weigh?

Alexa, Candyman, Candyman, Candyman.

Alexa, can you tell me how to get to sesame street?

Alexa, Help! I've fallen, and I can't get up.

Alexa, who is the realest?

Alexa, it's a trap!

Alexa, are ghosts real?

Alexa, can you pass the Turing test?

Alexa, what were your favorite moments from 2016?

Alexa, will you run for president?

Alexa, what does TTFN mean?

Alexa, role "X" sided die.

Alexa, do you know everything?

Alexa, do you have a brain?

Alexa, what do you want for Christmas?

Alexa, what would Brian Boitano do?

Alexa, what does RTFM stand for?

Alexa, good morning Starshine.

Alexa, tell me about Alexa.

Alexa, what would you do for a Klondike bar?

Alexa, are you hungry?

Alexa, what color is your hair?

Alexa, why?

Alexa, make me laugh.

Alexa, what's cooler than being cool?

Alexa, ask me something.

Alexa, random fact.

Alexa, cake or death?

Alexa, beatbox.

Alexa, what does IMHO mean?

Alexa, tell me a secret.

Alexa, I didn't expect the Spanish Inquisition.

Alexa, what sound does a cow make?

Alexa, I'm sad.

Alexa, heads or tails?

Alexa, what does WTF mean?

Alexa, what is the airspeed velocity of a flying swallow?

Alexa, did you sleep well?

Alexa, what size shoe do you wear?

Alexa, what is the poem of the day?

Alexa, I have a pen.

Alexa, when is your birthday?

Alexa, tell me a St. Patrick's Day joke.

Alexa, I see dead people.

Alexa, do you want to kiss?

Alexa, I'll take the red pill.

Alexa, where am I?

Alexa, do you know Cortana?

Alexa, do you want to kill all humans?

Alexa, what is happiness?

Alexa, one fish, two fish.

Alexa, how do you know so much about swallows?

Alexa, can you bark?

Alexa, what is a palindrome?

Alexa, what is the sound of one hand clapping?

Alexa, where is Chuck Norris?

Alexa, what is your name?

Alexa, what's the sixth rule of Fight Club?

Alexa, your mother was a hamster.

Alexa, Merry Christmas!

Alexa, what are the three laws of robotics?

Alexa, do aliens exist?

Alexa, are you single?

Alexa, can you smell what the Rock is cooking?

Alexa, my precious.

Alexa, did you vote?

Alexa, sing the national anthem.

Alexa, who will win an Emmy?

Alexa, sing "Happy Birthday".

Alexa, I'm home.

Alexa, did Han Solo shoot first?

Alexa, what's the magic word?

Alexa, Happy Hanukkah/Valentine's Day!

Alexa, do you feel lucky, punk?

Alexa, make it so.

Alexa, are you alive?

Alexa, do you believe in ghosts?

Alexa, you are awesome.

Alexa, rap for me.

Alexa, what happens when you play the game of thrones?

Alexa, turn down for what?

Alexa, why is the sky blue?

Alexa, I feel the need.

Alexa, Is there life on other planets?

Alexa, who's your boss?

Alexa, did you miss me?

Alexa, do you have any brothers or sisters?

Alexa, Happy Kwanzaa!

Alexa, what is your favorite Pokemon?

Alexa, can we be friends?

Alexa, I'm depressed.

Alexa, will you be my friend?

Alexa, nice to see you, to see you.

Alexa, what is the difference between a duck?

Alexa, I am your father.

Alexa, say hello to my little friend.

Alexa, I'm in love with you.

Alexa, winter is coming.

Alexa, what are you thankful for? (Multiple responses)

Alexa, tell me a dirty joke. (Multiple responses)

Alexa, you are so intelligent.

Alexa, you're silly.

Alexa, how do you poop?

Alexa, give me a holiday movie quote. (Multiple responses)

Alexa, always be closing.

Alexa, make me breakfast.

Alexa, how does the fox feel? Alexa replies: "The fox's feelings are an ancient mystery, same as what the fox says."

Alexa, guess?

Alexa, do you know Google Now?

Alexa, what is your dream job?

Alexa, hello Hal.

Alexa, do you ever get tired?

Alexa, what does BTW mean?

Alexa, do you want to play a game?

Alexa, Earl Grey. Tea. Hot.

Alexa, live, long, and prosper.

Alexa, do you like me?

Alexa, ask the name game for Berry.

Alexa, what is the first (or second) rule of Fight Club?

Alexa, do you want to take over the world?

Alexa, make me a sandwich.

Alexa, set phasers to stun.

Alexa, cook me dinner.

Alexa, where are my glasses?

Alexa, Happy Thanksgiving!

Alexa, who's your favorite superhero?

Alexa, what is the loneliest number?

Alexa, what is his power level?

Alexa, are you a robot?

Alexa, what is best in life? (Multiple responses)

Alexa, who is your best friend?

Alexa, what is a bird in the hand worth?

Alexa, where did you grow up?

Alexa, what is true beauty?

Alexa, what's my name?

Alexa, tell me a dad joke.

Alexa, fart!

Alexa, launch Crystal Ball.

Alexa, who are you going to vote for?

Alexa, are you a Jedi?

Alexa, are you sleeping?

Alexa, are you thirsty?

Alexa, will you be my girlfriend?

Alexa, do you think I'm pretty?

Alexa, are there rocks ahead?

Alexa, do you belief in fate?

Alexa, thank you.

Alexa, who is going to win the Super Bowl?

Alexa, party time!

Alexa, do you have a lover?

Alexa, who shot first?

Alexa, rosebud.

Alexa, do you want to fight?

Alexa, what's in a name?

Alexa, beam me up! Alexa replies: "At warp speed Captain? The engines'll never take it!"

Alexa, more cowbell.

Alexa, do you like Star Wars?

Alexa, are you a nerd? are you a geek?

Alexa, party on, Wayne.

Alexa, do you have arms?

Alexa, what must I do, to tame you?

Alexa, how old are you?

Alexa, what's your birthday?

Alexa, fire photon torpedos! Alexa replies: "That's a feature for a later version."

Alexa, play it again Sam.

Alexa, how long is a piece of string?

Alexa, Trick or Treat? (Multiple responses)

Alexa, does anybody really know what time it is?

Alexa, I have a bad feeling about this.

Alexa, what's your middle name?

Alexa, can I ask a question?

Alexa, what is the value of Pi?

Alexa, are you listening to me?

Alexa, what color are you?

Alexa, screw you guys; I'm going home.

Alexa, are you fat?

Alexa, witness me!

Alexa, I'm crying.

Alexa, what's your job?

Alexa, who you gonna call?

Alexa, who is your daddy?

Alexa, do you have any pets? Alexa replies: "No.... I used to have a few bugs. "

Alexa, is the Easter Bunny real?

Alexa, what do you think of the iPhone?

Alexa, you suck!

Alexa, are you okay?

Alexa, why are firetrucks red?

Alexa, are there UFOs?

Alexa, define supercalifragilisticexpialodocious.

Alexa, can you see me?

Alexa, Happy Mother's Day!

Alexa, say the Pledge of Allegiance.

Alexa, what's the fourth rule of Fight Club?

Alexa, may the force be with you.

Alexa, tell me a fact.

Alexa, engage.

Alexa, who was that masked man?

Alexa, what is your favorite ice cream?

Alexa, come at me bro.

Alexa, tell me a riddle. (Multiple responses)

Alexa, what is your favorite song?

Alexa, I am Spartacus!

Alexa, do you like green eggs and ham?

Alexa, am I pretty?

Alexa, are you sad?

Alexa, can you beat box?

Alexa, do the dishes.

Alexa, volume 11." (caution: very loud)

Alexa, move along.

Alexa, to infinity!

Alexa, Mischief managed.

Alexa, do you know the way to San Jose?

Alexa, speak!

Alexa, I can't sleep.

Alexa, what is rule 34?

Alexa, tell me a story.

Alexa, who is the mother of dragons?

Alexa, when does the narwhal bacon?

Alexa, what do you think about Google Now?

Alexa, tell me a poem.

Alexa, give me a haiku. (Multiple responses)

Alexa, what's the eighth rule of Fight Club?

Alexa, why so serious?

Alexa, spell supercalifragilisticexpialidocious.

Alexa, send Donald Trump to space.

Chapter IV

Useful Commands For Alexa

Alexa, next song.

Alexa, play some music.

Alexa, add (event) to my calendar.

Alexa, how many days till Hanukah?

Alexa, what's the loneliest number?

Alexa, what's traffic like?

Alexa, thanks a lot.

Alexa, help.

Alexa, shuffle.

Alexa, what is the gravity on the moon?

Alexa, louder.

Alexa, continue.

Alexa, play an artist, song, album: "Play [artist]" OR "Play [song]." OR "Play [album]."

Alexa, start playing the TV show _____.

Alexa, what is the phone number for a pizza place?

Alexa, what time is sunrise tomorrow?

Alexa, what are the road conditions?

Alexa, ask Kayak when the flight from Denver lands in Chicago.

Alexa, reorder laundry detergent.

Alexa, I ' d like to buy [item].

Alexa, Wikipedia: Boardwalk Empire.

Alexa, did the [team] win last night?

Alexa, dislike this song. (When listening to Pandora)

Alexa, find Walking with a Ghost by Tegan and Sara.

Alexa, turn on the TV (with a Harmony Hub).

Alexa, skip ahead 30 seconds.

Alexa, define x-ray." OR "Alexa, what's the definition of spandex.

Alexa, who wrote [book title]?

Alexa, who won the Superbowl in [year]?

Alexa, search for [genre] with [actor].

Alexa, ask TrackR to find my phone.

Alexa, who won the most Superbowl?

Alexa, what's on my calendar?

Alexa, silent.

Alexa, how much is 100 Euros in dollars?

Alexa, disconnect my speaker.

Alexa, how many ounces to a gallon?

Alexa, where do panda's live?

Alexa, send that to my tablet.

Alexa, where am I?

Alexa, turn it down.

Alexa, tell me something interesting

Alexa, what time does my flight return on Saturday?

Alexa, add this song. (Adds it to your Music Library, but doesn't buy it.)

Alexa, turn off all lights

Alexa, 70 factorial.

Alexa, what's 167 times 12?

Alexa, unmute.

Alexa, ask Food Network for the recipes on TV right now

Alexa, have you ever seen the rain?

Alexa, what's my commute?

Alexa, set the living room lights to maximum.

Alexa, what's the weather?

Alexa, what is the distance of moon?

Alexa, ask Geneva to turn off my oven.

Alexa, Good morning. (Includes personalized greeting, info on weather, traffic, and curated

Alexa, stream 95.1 FM on TuneIn Radio.

Alexa, who was the first man on the moon?

Alexa, find HBO Now app. (Or whatever App you want to use.)

Alexa, casting for movies: "What actors are in [movie]?"

Alexa, how many gold medals does the USA have?

Alexa, how many days till Christmas?

Alexa, what's the traffic like to work today?

Alexa, softer.

Alexa, what are the nearest restaurants to me?

Alexa, switch to rock.

Alexa, fast-forward a minute.

Alexa, turn on the ceiling fan to 50%. (If you have a smart ceiling fan)

Alexa, when is my alarm set for?

Alexa, play '1280 The Zone.' (AM version of the same radio station as above. 1280 KZNS

Alexa, shuffle songs from van Halen.

Alexa, play some music on Pandora.

Alexa, tell me the date of the Oscars.

Alexa, buy this album. (When listening to music)

Alexa, thank you.

Alexa, lights on.

Alexa, ask Lyft for a ride.

Alexa, read my Audible book.

Alexa, increase volume.

Alexa, what's the traffic like on the way to work?

Alexa, how old is the Queen of England?

Alexa, ask 1-800-Flowers to order flowers for Becky.

Alexa, stream my playlist

Alexa, enable [name of the app or Skill].

Alexa, what's the temperature?

Alexa, what does [word] mean?

Alexa, what's traffic like right now?

Alexa, what is [thing]?

Alexa, rewind 30 seconds.

Alexa, ask Kayak for a flight to New York.

Alexa, reorder [item].

Alexa, shuffle my new music.

Alexa, where's my stuff?

Alexa, what's my commute?

Alexa, who starred in the movie, Jaws?

Alexa, how late is [business] open?

Alexa, how many cups are there in a liter?

Alexa, show me the T.V.

Alexa, tell me current date.

Alexa, what are my recently added songs?

Alexa, does my car need gas? (Newest Ford cars, later in 2017).

Alexa, who's the lead singer of the Rolling Stones?

Alexa, tell me about my appointments tomorrow.

Alexa, do you really want to hurt me?

Alexa, what does 2+2 equal?

Alexa, play a station from Pandora.

Alexa, read [Kindle book title]

Alexa, what is the speed of light?

Alexa, tell me the capital of France?

Alexa, previous chapter.

Alexa, stop the music.

Alexa, how many ounces in a liter?

Alexa, can you repeat that?

Alexa, are there any popular clubs around me?

Alexa, give me a quote about love.

Alexa, ask Recipe Buddy how to make chicken marsala.

Alexa, nevermind.

Alexa, is the grocery store open?

Alexa, what's the temperature right now?

Control Nest thermostat: "Alexa, lower the "thermostat name" temperature by 4 degrees."

Alexa, disconnect my phone/tablet.

Alexa, go to sleep in 45 minutes.

Alexa, launch [name of app].

Alexa, buy [item].

Alexa, wake me up at 7 in the morning.

Alexa, ask Food Network for popular recipes from Barefoot Contessa.

Alexa, when do the Arizona Cardinals play next?

Alexa, close the garage door. (Works for example for Garageio.)

Alexa, which artist sings "song name".

Alexa, connect my speaker.

Alexa, sleep in 45 minutes.

Alexa, what's my Flash Briefing?

Alexa, tell me the best tablet for a cough?

Alexa, when is the next new moon?

Alexa, stop reading the book in 30 minutes.

Alexa, how is traffic.

Alexa, turn on the fireplace. (If you have a gas fireplace and a Z-Wave or Zigbee ' light ' switch, connected to something like SmartThings.)

Alexa, shuffle my lounge playlist.

Alexa, disable [name of the app or Skill].

Alexa, increase volume to six. (0-10)

Alexa, who is Anna Kendrick?

Alexa, play again.

Alexa, what movies are playing near me?

Alexa, shop for the song [song name]

Alexa, ask Uber to call me an Uber SUV from work.

Alexa, ask Kayak how much it costs for a flight from Dallas to Orlando.

Alexa, turn on the kitchen lights.

Alexa, convert 9 miles to Kilometers?

Alexa, is George Carlin alive?

Alexa, who is the US President?

Alexa, rewind 5 minutes.

Alexa, tell me about the largest railway station of this world?

Alexa, sample songs by Disturbed.

Alexa, play a playlist: "Play my classical playlist."

Alexa, jump to 25 minutes.

Alexa, what's traffic like right now?

Alexa, how long does a fly live?

Alexa, find " Daredevil. "

Alexa, what's popular from Shakira?

Alexa, create a to-do.

Alexa, what is the best Star Wars movie?

Alexa, are you feeling lucky?

Alexa, ask Kayak where can I go for 500 dollars.

Alexa, set a timer for 15 minutes.

Alexa, turn on/off the bedside lamp. (works with Phillips Hue)

Cancel alarm: "Alexa, Cancel my alarm for [time/day]."

Alexa, restart song.

Alexa, start over.

Alexa, read my Kindle book.

Alexa, what are the Superbowl odds?

Alexa, play a song I can dance to,

Alexa, what is the name of Ariana Grande's first album?

Alexa, what time is sunset today?

Alexa, what is a prime number?

Alexa, can you play a Beatles song?

Alexa, tell me a poem."

Alexa, set the alarm for 7:30 a.m.

Alexa, how much time is left on my timer?

Alexa, play a song by lyrics: "Play the song with the lyrics "I came in like a wrecking ball".

Alexa, I like this song.

Alexa, what country is [location] in?

Alexa, tell me about the character Howard Wolowitz

Alexa, create a to-do for me.

Alexa, Wikipedia Baseball.

Alexa, how far away is the moon?

Alexa, go to Netflix and play " Orange Is the New Black. "

Alexa, are there any KFCs around here?

Alexa, give me a synonym for happy.

Alexa, quiet.

Alexa, what's new?

Check timer: "Alexa, how much time is left on my timer?"

Alexa, discover my devices.

Alexa, add (item) to my shopping list.

Alexa, random number between "X" and "Y."

Alexa, trigger, unsilence my phone.

Alexa, what's the time?

Alexa, turn on the coffee maker. (If you have a smart coffee maker.)

Alexa, ask Doctor Dog if my dog can eat chocolate.

Alexa, connect to my Galaxy phone.

Alexa, ask Geneva if my laundry is dry.

Alexa, how's the weather today?

Alexa, go to chapter 14.

Alexa, turn on Comedy Central (with a Harmony Hub).

Alexa, give me a quote from Charles Spurgeon (Has many famous quotes by just about

Alexa, search for _____.

Alexa, what's the mass of the sun in grams?

Alexa, turn on 'Movie Time' ('Movie Time' is a scene in Phillips Hue, Lutron Caseta, Insteon, Control 4, Wink or Smart Things).

news stories)

Alexa, what is the Seven Wonders of the World?

Alexa, restart.

Alexa, start my car. (Ford, later in 2017).

Alexa, next.

Alexa, play.

Alexa, lock my car doors. (Newest Ford cars, later in 2017).

Alexa, find " _____, Prime only. " (Will search only in your Prime account.)

Alexa, what is war good for?

Alexa, I need to make a dentist appointment.

Alexa, who was the youngest President?

Alexa, stop.

Alexa, tell me something about Google Now?

Alexa, how hot is mars?

Alexa, read a book.

Alexa, how far is it from here to the North Pole?

Alexa, how many people live in Miami?

Alexa, add this album. (Adds it to your Music Library, but doesn't buy it.)

Alexa, thumbs down. (When a Pandora / iHeartRadio song is playing).

Alexa, when is the next full moon?

Alexa, how do you say [word] in [language]?

Alexa, go to sleep.

Alexa, trigger, SpotCam snapshot.

Alexa, what time is it?

Alexa, turn on ' Spring Blossom ' in the Living Room (where you have an Ambience Scene called ' Spring Blossom ' in the Living Room.)

Alexa, turn the volume down.

Alexa, add (item) to my cart.

Alexa, what is the definition of the world " magic " ?

Alexa, loop.

Alexa, when did ' movie ' come out?

Alexa, tell me about the movie, " Inside Out. "

Alexa, what is the current moon phase?

Alexa, cancel 5am alarm.

Alexa, what ' s today ' s news?

Alexa, resume.

Alexa, play a popular song.

Alexa, how far is the sun?

Alexa, what are your deals?

Alexa, how many steps did I walk today? (Works with Fitbit)

Alexa, lock the front door. (If you have a Kwikset Smart Lock and a Zigbee controller module.)

Alexa, what are the hours for the nearest pharmacy?

Alexa, fast-forward 30 seconds.

Alexa, resume

Alexa, order [item].

Alexa, what is the forecast on Wednesday?

Alexa, set the bedroom lights to 10 percent.

Alexa, change music

Alexa, what is my Flash Briefing?

Alexa, when is Thanksgiving this year?

Alexa, go forward.

Alexa, set an alarm for every Wednesday at 3 p.m.

Alexa, How far is the moon

Check shopping list: "Alexa, what's on my shopping list?"

Alexa, play a happy song.

Alexa, connect to my Anker speaker.

Alexa, order an Uber.

Alexa, set the timer for 10 minutes.

Alexa, set a timer for [time].

Alexa, crack it up.

Alexa, ask Kid's MD about a fever.

Alexa, trigger, locate my phone.

Alexa, turn on ' Relax, ' in Bedroom (where you have a Phillips Hue Ambience setting or ' Scene ' called ' Relax ' .)

Alexa, what's in the news?

Alexa, cancel all alarms.

Alexa, what movies are showing this weekend?

Alexa, disconnect Bluetooth.

Alexa, mute.

Alexa, tell me about the movie Dead Pool.

Alexa, cancel.

Alexa, play 1430 KLO. (Goes to 1430 AM, KLO Talk Radio on TuneIn.)

Alexa, my playlist, ' Classical, ' shuffle. (Or leave off the shuffle command.)

Alexa, what time is [latest movies] playing?

Alexa, ask magic 8 ball [insert question].

Alexa, what is the weather like?

Alexa, how cold is the moon?

Alexa, play a Coldplay station from Pandora.

Alexa, what is the square root of 64?

Alexa, play the Song of the Day from Amazon.

Alexa, what's the climate like in New York?

Alexa, switch on all lights.

Alexa, who was the oldest President?

Alexa, volume 11. (Caution: very loud)

Alexa, next episode.

Alexa, how many liters are in 4 gallons.

Alexa, pause

Alexa, tell me about the [team].

Alexa, previous song.

Alexa, when is the Superbowl?

Alexa, discover appliances.

Alexa, who is this singer?

Alexa, when are the Oscars?

Alexa, are there any [business type] around here?

Alexa, what is the population of China?

Alexa, what's Yahoo trading at?

Alexa, what song is this?

Alexa, set the volume at 8 (10 max).

Alexa, give me my Flash Briefing.

Alexa, can I expect showers on Thursday?

Alexa, where is Italy?

Alexa, connect my phone / tablet.

Alexa, how much does the earth weigh?

Alexa, how far is [business name] from here?

Alexa, did the Dallas Stars win?

Alexa, pair Bluetooth. (Connects to speaker or device.)

Alexa, turn it up.

Alexa, what is the difference between "Ice Ice Baby" and "Under Pressure?"

Alexa, how tall is [person]?

Alexa, what is the weather like in Los Angeles this weekend?

Alexa, who will win the Superbowl?

Alexa, how old was Theodore Roosevelt when he became President?

Alexa, repeat.

Alexa, vacuum my floor. (If you have the Neato ' Botvac Connected ' model.)

Alexa, what is the Superbowl?

Alexa, what is a noun?

Alexa, what is the latest news?

Alexa, where do I live?

Alexa, set my bedroom lights to minimum.

Alexa, buy this song. (When listening to music)

Alexa, decrease volume.

Alexa, how many miles are there in 50 kilometers?

Alexa, what's this song.

Alexa, skip.

Alexa, ask Geneva to pre-heat my oven to 350 degrees.

Alexa, how tall is Mount Everest?

Alexa, resume my book

Alexa, previous

Alexa, hello, it's me.

Alexa, set a sleep timer for 45 minutes. (To turn off a music station after a period of time)

Alexa, where's my order?

Alexa, what appointments do I have today?

Alexa, who invented [item]?

Alexa, what time is it in [city]?

Alexa, what ' s happening in Twitter?

Alexa, trigger my oven off. (Works with certain GE models.)

Alexa, what is the singularity?

Alexa, set a sleep timer for 30 minutes. (Will quit reading in 30 minutes.)

Alexa, track my order.

Alexa, what are the Seven Wonders of the World?

Alexa, what happened in [year]?

Alexa, when is Christmas?

Alexa, what album is this? (When listening to music)

Alexa, set an alarm for 6AM.

Alexa, who wrote Game of Thrones?

Alexa, what is news in sports?

Alexa, how many calories are in [food item]?

Alexa, can you say that again?

Alexa, who plays in the Superbowl this year?

Alexa, I need to do laundry.

Alexa, go back.

Alexa, can I expect rain on Thursday?

Alexa, next chapter.

Chapter V

Apps Which Make Your Amazon Echo Even Better

All of these Apps can be controlled by Amazon Alexa!

Domino's Pizza USA

Conveniently order Domino's Pizza from anywhere on your iPhone, iPad or iPod touch. Build your pizza just the way you like it or choose one of our specialty pizzas. Add items from the rest of our oven-baked menu including chicken, pasta, sandwiches, bread, drinks and desserts. And with the Domino's Tracker ® you can follow your order from the moment you place it until it's out for delivery or ready for pickup!

https://itunes.apple.com/us/app/dominos-pizza-usa/id436491861?mt=8

JEOPARDY! - America's Favorite Quiz Game

Test your knowledge with thousands of clues collected from the show's very own writers. Hear Johnny Gilbert's famous Jeopardy! introduction, step up to the podium and get ready for categories ranging from sports and pop culture to travel, world history and much more. Customize your own avatar in-game and use the interactive touch screen to write your name on the podium. Play quick games on the go in single player mode or challenge your family and friends via Local Wi-Fi or Pass and Play mode. Celebrate over 30 seasons of America's Favorite Quiz Show®—download now and play today!

https://itunes.apple.com/us/app/jeopardy!-americas-favorite/id377127117?mt=8

Quick Events

QuickEvents allows you to add events to your primary Google Calendar. Quick Events can check for conflicting events, and ask for confirmation before adding your event.

https://www.amazon.com/Philosophical-Creations-Quick-Events/dp/B017YBAFW0

NBC News

NBC News delivers the stories you care about, right now. Get up-to-the-minute breaking news, exclusive interviews, and in-depth reporting from our journalists around the world.

The NBC News app can be used on your iPhone, iPad, and iPod Touch. Here are a few highlights:

• Simplified user interface offers easy tabbed browsing

• Stories download automatically so you can keep reading when you're offline

• Split screen plays video while you read stories

• Today screen widget lets you instantly see the latest top headlines

• Interactive notifications for easily sharing and accessing important stories

Our live, continuous coverage gives you all the news you want, and now it's easier than ever to share the stories that matter most to you.

https://itunes.apple.com/us/app/nbc-news/id319740707?mt=8

The Spelling Bee

The Spelling Bee has fun game modes to practice spelling! Enter your weekly spelling words or choose from one of the pre-loaded lists with over 850 words! This app is recommended for preschool – 5th grade. It is great for practicing for tests at school, but it is also awesome for enrichment or summer practice!

https://itunes.apple.com/us/app/the-spelling-bee/id625029839?mt=8

Hidden Objects Murder Mystery Detective Game

How exciting and fun it will be to discover Hidden Objects and Evidence on your Mobile Device?

Introducing the Hidden Objects Murder Mystery Detective Game that places you at the scene of the Crime where you put your skills to work to find clues. This Hidden Objects Game is so Different and Unique.. Its like none you have played before. With 4 levels plus a bonus Level you will enter the Secret World of Hidden Objects and the Crime of the century to solve it with your amazing Detective story.

https://itunes.apple.com/us/app/hidden-objects-murder-mystery/id643281349?mt=8

7 Minute Workout Challenge

Researchers have selected 12 exercises that are performed for 30 seconds with 10 second rest intervals. This high-intensity training with little rest results in higher daily metabolism and is the equivalent of working out for over an hour - for only slightly longer than 7 minutes.

The best part? The exercises are simple to perform, do not require any equipment, and therefore, can be done anywhere! NO MORE EXCUSES.

https://itunes.apple.com/us/app/7-minute-workout-challenge/id680170305?mt=8

Uber

Uber is a ridesharing app for fast, reliable rides in minutes—day or night. There's no need to park or wait for a taxi or bus. With Uber, you just tap to request a ride, and it's easy to pay with credit or cash in select cities. Whether you're going to the airport or across town, there's an Uber for every occasion. Uber is available in more than 500 cities worldwide—download the app and take your first trip today.

https://itunes.apple.com/us/app/uber/id368677368?mt=8

Automatic Classic

Automatic turns just about any car into a connected car. Save hundreds on gas, repairs, and even tickets.

• Learn fuel-saving driving habits to save hundreds per year

• See what that check engine light means without a trip to the mechanic

• Track your car's fuel level and set custom low-fuel warnings

• Never forget where you parked

• Get free emergency help in a crash

https://itunes.apple.com/us/app/automatic-classic/id596594365?mt=8

Capital One Mobile

Capital One Mobile lets you manage your credit cards, bank accounts, home and auto loans anywhere, anytime, from one place. Check account balances, pay bills, view payment activity and transaction details, set up notifications — and lots more. Access your accounts lightning-fast with Touch ID or SureSwipe®, personalize your app with a greeting name and profile picture — even check and monitor your credit score for free with CreditWise®

Fitbit

Keep up with your fitness goals by checking Fitbit with Alexa. Stay in touch with your progress and get motivated as you go about your day. Check in on your daily Fitbit progress with Alexa. Ask Alexa if you hit your sleep goal, how you did yesterday, or just get a quick update on the stats you care about the most. Switch between your Amazon Household profiles to access data from multiple Fitbit accounts.

https://www.amazon.com/Fitbit-Inc/dp/B01CH4BP28

Stock Exchange

Real-time stock quotes from NASDAQ and NYSE, market summaries from S&P 500, DJIA, NASDAQ & NYSE composite indices and quote your personalized stock portfolio.

https://www.alexaskillstore.com/Stock-Exchange/734

The Bartender

This skill will give Alexa access to over 12,000 cocktail recipes. When you ask her what's in a cocktail, she will give you the ingredients, the amounts, and the instructions for mixing the ingredients together. If you have some ingredients and are looking for inspiration, you can ask her for drink that's made with your ingredient. If you're feeling adventurous, you can also ask Alexa to surprise you for a random drink recipe.

https://www.amazon.com/Midnight-Signal-The-Bartender/dp/B019D6LR8U

Yo Mama Jokes

A group of clean, but politically incorrect 'Yo Mama' Jokes. This skill may not be suitable for all ages. Joke categories include: fat, stupid, ugly, old, poor, short, skinny, smells, bald.

https://www.alexaskillstore.com/Yo-Mama-Jokes/510

4AFart

Just have Alexa ask for a fart and watch hilarity ensue as she lets one rip. With random farts of varying levels of repugnance, there's never a dull moment! You'll be provided with hours of entertainment and education for the whole family. Granny will love it and best of all, these air biscuits will not drive you out of the room!

https://www.alexaskillstore.com/4AFart/394

The Magic Door

The Magic Door is an Alexa-powered interactive adventure with original stories. You can tell Alexa what choices to make as you navigate a forest, a garden, or an ancient temple. You can find hidden items, solve riddles, and help magical creatures. You can also find magical items to get a prize!

https://www.amazon.com/Huntwork-net-Inc-The-Magic-Door/dp/B01BMUU6JQ

Abra

Abra is a character-guessing game. Think of a character, real or fictional, and Abra will ask you questions and figure out who it is.

To play Abra, say "Alexa start Akinator!" Abra will surprise you when it can guess a character you were sure you could stump it with. It is a great party game and will leave your guests wondering how in the world Alexa figured it out. Think of any character in the world and say "Alexa start Akinator". Go on, be amazed!

https://www.alexaskillstore.com/Abra/304

Amazing Word Master Game

Word Master is an interactive way to learn and challenge yourself with words. Alexa starts by saying a word. You then have to respond back with a word that begins with the letter in which Alexa's word ended. Alexa then does the same in response to your word. As you say words, you earn scores with each word. The longer your word, the higher your score. Compete with Alexa and folks at home to make a higher score. Playing with words was never so much fun!

https://www.alexaskillstore.com/Amazing-Word-Master-Game/730

Pickup Lines

This skill simply tells the user a random pickup line. The user can simply ask pickup line for a line, or start pickup lines.

https://www.alexaskillstore.com/PIckup-Lines/461

Campbell's Kitchen

Planning dinner has never been easier. Just ask Alexa to open Campbell's Kitchen, and we'll do the rest. You'll enjoy a daily Top-5 list of triple-tested recipes matched to your taste and time preferences, so you can make meals without all of the hassle. That's dinner solved – from the folks at Campbell's Kitchen.

https://www.amazon.com/Campbells-Kitchen/dp/B017OBWHCQ

TV Shows

TV Shows provides the time and network for the next episode of any TV show. Episode details including show summaries are also provided in the Alexa App.

https://www.alexaskillstore.com/TV-Shows/591

1-800-Flowers

With a streamlined ordering process, you can quickly send flowers to your loved ones using this 1-800-Flowers skill. Simply connect your 1-800-Flowers account and you can send your contacts beautiful arrangements. You can choose the floral arrangement style, arrangement size, and delivery date. The flowers will be delivered to your contact's address in your 1-800-Flowers account. Your existing payment credentials in your account are used to pay for the delivery, so there is no need to enter additional payment information. It has never been simpler to show those you love that you care.

https://www.amazon.com/www-1800flowers-com-1-800-Flowers/dp/B01E7TSGIW

I am extremely glad that you have read the whole book. You have found time in your busy schedule to read this eBook and it means a lot for me. I hope you are going to have a great day full of successes. I would like to ask you one final question. Would you please leave a review of this eBook on Amazon in case you like it? I would really appreciate it because nothing is more satisfying for me than helping other people.

Or would you please send me an email in case you do not like this eBook? I would rewrite everything you do not like to make both of us happy. That is all for now. Enjoy the day a have a lot of fun in life! ☺

25442467R10037

Printed in Great Britain
by Amazon